ALPHABET RIDDLES

Susan Joyce

illustrations by
Doug DuBosque

PEEL PRODUCTIONS, INC.

For Gloria — thank you for being a
patient teacher.

—SJ

For M'Lou — thanks for the support
and encouragement.

—DD

Text copyright©1998 Susan Joyce

Illustrations & design
copyright©1998 Doug DuBosque

All rights reserved.

Published by
Peel Productions, Inc.
PO Box 546
Columbus NC 28722
http://peelbooks.com

Printed & bound in Hong Kong

L_____y of Congress
Cataloging-in-publication data

Joyce, Susan, 1945–
    Alphabet riddles / by Susan Joyce ;
illustrations by Doug DuBosque
    p.   cm.
    Summary: Presents riddles in rhyme for
each letter of the alphabet.
    ISBN 0-939217-50-3 (trade)
    1. Riddles, Juvenile. [1. Riddles. 2.
Alphabet.] I. DuBosque, D. C., ill. II. Title.

PN6371.5.J68 1998
793'.735--dc21
[E]   97-43676

a p r o n

I start with an A and end with an N.

I'm something you wear

when you're stuffing a hen,

or cooking a steak,

or icing a cake, or

mixing a shake.

Can you name me?

b__l

I start with a B and end with an L.

You can kick me or throw me,

and bounce me as well.

If you hit me and run,

the fans will have fun.

What do you think I can be? Can you tell?

c_p

I start with a C and end with a P.

I'm round, with a handle.

You drink out of me.

Fill me with juice,

or with peppermint tea.

Or YOUR favorite drink.

What can I be?

d__l

I start with a D and end with an L.

I come in all sizes,

and colors as well.

Hold my hand and I'll walk.

Pull my string and I'll talk.

What do you think I can be? Can you tell?

e___o

I start with an E and end with an O.

I'm a sound that repeats.

I bounce back and grow.

When you say, "Hello."

I say, "Hel-lo-lo-lo."

What can I possibly be? Do you know?

f__g

I start with an F and end with a G.

My colors and stripes identify me.

On my pole, I fly high,

As I wave in the sky.

What in the world can I possibly be?

g–_t

I start with a G and end with a T.

I'm something you like to receive.

(And I'm free!)

A bike or a ball. A book or a doll.

You can wish for them all!

What can I be?

h_g

I start with a H and end with a G.

When someone is sad, I make them happy.

Give a hold, or a squeeze,

with your arms. (Not your knees!)

What in the world do you think I can be?

i_e

I start with an I and end with an E.

I'll stand still or run,

until you freeze me.

Skate on me in the rink.

Let me help cool your drink.

What do you think? Can you name me?

j_ _ _e

I start with a J and end with an E.

I'm something you tell to your friends.

(I'm funny!)

They'll giggle and squiggle,

and wiggle with glee.

They'll laugh and laugh.

What can I be?

k__e

I start with a K and end with an E.

My bright colors fly

on a string you can't see.

I do tricks in the sky,

when the wind carries me.

What in the world can I possibly be?

l__s

I start with an L and end with an S.

You use me to whisper,

you use me to kiss.

I help trumpeters blow,

both high notes and low.

What can I possibly be?

(Do you know?)

m__k

I start with an M, and end with a K.

I'm fun to have on,

but not every day.

Look funny or mean...

...on stage? Halloween?

What can I possibly be? Can you say?

n___e

I start with an N, and end with an E.

You use me to smell,

you use me to breathe.

I run, but don't walk.

I'm above where you talk.

What can I be? Can you name me?

o____n

I start with an O and end with an N.

At the edge of the beach

is where I begin.

I'm home to the whale,

and big ships that sail.

What in the world can I be? Can you tell?

p_t

I start with a P and end with a T.

Dog, cat or hamster,

please take care of me.

Treat me nice, I might purr.

Treat me rough, I might grrrrr.

A snake or a gerbil....

What can I be?

q___t

I start with a Q and end with a T.

I'm colorful, big,

and warm as can be.

Sold in stores and at fairs,

I'm a patchwork of squares.

What in the world can I possibly be?

r_____n

I start with an R and end with an N.

Sometimes I'm wide.

Sometimes I'm thin.

You'll feel really proud

when I'm something you win.

What in the world do you think I am?

s__k

I start with an S and end with a K.

Buy me in bright colors,

or just plain old gray.

I come in a pair, and

I'm something to wear.

(But not in your hair!)

What am I? Can you say?

t_____n

I start with a T and end with an N.

Watch me! Listen!

I'm quite an invention.

I beam sounds and faces,

from faraway places.

What can I possibly be?

What's my name?

u_____a

I start with a U and end with an A.

I'll give you some shade,

on the beach where you play.

And I'll keep you dry

on a wet, rainy day.

What do you think I can be? Can you say?

v_____e

I start with a V and end with an E.

I'm something you send

to friends or family.

On one special day,

with the message, PLEASE BE...

Hope you'll BE MINE!

Can you name me?

w_ _ _d

I start with a W; end with a D.

I touch every house,

every rock, every tree.

I'm warm and I'm friendly,

or cold as can be.

I blow in your face. What can I be?

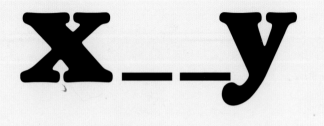

x__y

I start with an X and end with a Y.

I show buttons and bones.

I can't tell a lie.

Your doctor will know,

in the picture I show,

if you've broken your toe.

What am I?

y＿＿o

I start with a Y and end with an O.

Up, down, all around,

I can go fast or slow.

A toy on a string

I'm a round, simple thing.

What in the world can I be?

Do you know?

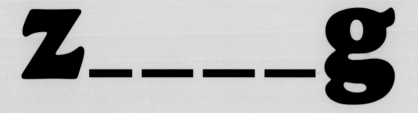

z_____g

I start with a Z and end with a G.

I move first one way, then turn abruptly.

Back and forth I go, like Zs in a row.

Do you possibly know?

Can you name me?

a_____s

We start with an A, and end with an S.

We say what's correct.

What did you guess?

turn the p__e

apron	hug	quilt
ball	ice	ribbon
cup	joke	sock
doll	kite	television
echo	lips	umbrella
flag	mask	valentine
gift	nose	zigzag
	pet	

Ideas for Parents and Teachers

~ Create your own word riddles! They don't need to be fancy.
  Start out simple:

>   I start with a C and end with a T.
>   I meow and yeow. What can I be?

~ Stretch the exercise: add more lines, with more clues.

~ In a group, instruct children to wait until all clues have been
  given before guessing the riddle. Have the child who guesses
  the answer first say the correct word, spell it out, and then
  make up a new riddle.

~ Encourage children to illustrate their riddles.

~ Share your best riddles with others!

Creating alphabet riddles that rhyme is a wonderful way to
explore words and what they mean. As you engage children
personally in the poetic process, you will see them blossom, both
in vocabulary and in their grasp of letters and sounds. Flexing
their "mental muscles" helps them develop reading, writing, and
thinking skills.

As a young child, I had dyslexia – and a very difficult time with
letters and words. My family encouraged me by making up
alphabet riddles. We would invent them while riding in the car,
waiting on a bus, or whenever we had a few minutes to spare.

Do the same! They're fun!

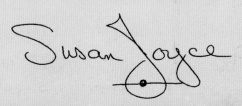

a_____t

I start with an A and end with a T.

You also could say I end with a Z.

I'm the symbols you use,

to write words you choose.

What in the world can I possibly be?